# THE 12 WORST
# FLOODS OF ALL TIME

by Laura Perdew

12 STORY LIBRARY

www.12StoryLibrary.com

12-Story Library is an imprint of Bookstaves.

Photographs ©: Steve Nicklas/NOAA, cover, 1; Smallegange; Luyken/PD, 4; Janwillemvanaalst/CC4.0, 5; Niday Picture Library/Alamy Stock Photo, 6; Rolfmueller/CC3.0, 7; Takayuki Hayato/Shutterstock.com, 8; Landsat-7/NASA, 9; Jocelyn Augustino/FEMA, 10; US Army, 11; Ricce/PD, 12; Ivo Bazzechi/PD, 13; Dennis Jarvis/CC2.0, 13; Chronicle/Alamy Stock Photo, 14; Le Grand Portage/CC2.0, 15; manhhai/Jim Comer/CC2.0, 17; Steve Nicklas/NOAA, 18; Steve Nicklas/NOAA, 19; PD, 20-22; Profshivajirao/PD, 23; SC National Guard/PD, 24; SC National Guard/PD, 25; PD, 26; Associated Press, 27; Brian A Jackson/Shutterstock.com, 28; 1000 Words/Shutterstock.com, 29

**ISBN**
978-1-63235-536-2 (hardcover)
978-1-63235-601-7 (paperback)
978-1-63235-655-0 (ebook)

**Library of Congress Control Number: 2018946728**

Printed in the United States of America
Mankato, MN
June 2018

About the Cover
The Great Mississippi Flood of 1927,
Arkansas City, Arkansas.

Access free, up-to-date content on this topic plus a full digital version of this book. Scan the QR code on page 31 or use your school's login at 12StoryLibrary.com.

# Table of Contents

# Netherlands City Lost After Massive Storm Surge

The Netherlands is a small country in northwest Europe along the North Sea. About half of its land area is less than 3.3 feet (1 m) above sea level. In fact, the word Netherlands means low country in Dutch. The nation has dikes, dams, and drainage systems to hold back water. This infrastructure is not always enough to prevent flooding.

On November 5, 1530, a large storm hit the Netherlands. It caused a massive storm surge from the North Sea. A wall of water rushed inland and washed away everything in its path. Whole villages disappeared. As many as 125,000 people lost their lives in the flooding.

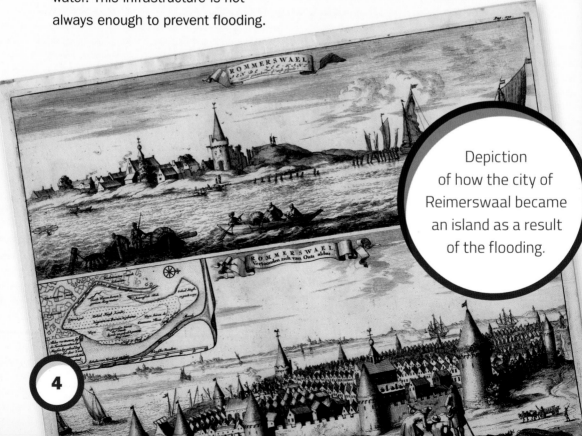

Depiction of how the city of Reimerswaal became an island as a result of the flooding.

The city of Reimerswaal sat a few feet higher than the surrounding area. It became an island. People tried to build new dams to hold back the water around the city. They wanted to reclaim the land that was lost. Nothing worked. The area around the city remained flooded. This led to the end of Reimerswaal. Isolated by water, residents deserted the city. Today the area is a salt marsh.

Map showing the area in the Netherlands that was affected by flooding.

## 18

**Number of villages washed away in the flood.**

- Much of the Netherlands lies at or below sea level.
- A storm surge on November 5, 1530, sent a wall of water inland.
- Up to 125,000 people died in the flooding.
- The flood led to Reimerswaal being deserted.

## THINK ABOUT IT

Before modern technology, how did people living by the North Sea build dikes and dams? How is technology being used today to prevent flooding? Research online to learn more.

# "China's Sorrow" Creates Widespread Destruction

The Yellow River in China is often called "China's Sorrow." This is because it has flooded more than a thousand times over two millennia. Yellow River floods have killed more people than any other river in the world.

For two thousand years, China has tried to tame the Yellow River. Dikes and dams have been built along the river. Channels have been created to protect farms and villages from high waters. These actions have not stopped the flooding. In fact, they have caused silt to build up in

Illustration of the 1887 flood.

the river bed. This has raised water levels. As a result, levees must be built higher. But the higher levees are built, the more dangerous floodwaters are in a breach.

Spillway of the Sanmenxia Dam on the Yellow River.

Floods in 1887 showed just how deadly the Yellow River could be. During September and October of that year, heavy rains fell. Dikes in the Henan province failed. Water poured over them into the low-lying plains below. Flooding covered 5,000 square miles (12,950 sq km) of land. This included 11 large towns and many more villages. Up to 2 million people lost their lives in the flood. Millions of others were left homeless. Farmlands were also destroyed.

## 3,000
### Miles (4,828 km) the Yellow River flows across China.

- The Chinese have tried to tame the Yellow River for centuries.
- Dikes and dams have been built to prevent flooding.
- In the fall of 1887, heavy rains fell, overflowing dikes in the Henan Province.
- Water poured into the plains below, destroying homes and farmlands.

## THINK ABOUT IT

Experts worry global warming will increase the number of catastrophic floods. How might this problem be addressed? Go online to learn how rising temperatures relate to flooding.

# Himalayan Quake Causes Floods in Asia's Indus Valley

In January 1841, an earthquake rocked the Himalayan mountains in Asia. The quake caused a rockslide on a peak called Nanga Parbat in the western part of the range. Falling debris blocked the flow of the Indus River. Water pooled behind this natural dam for months. At one point, the water was 500 feet (152 m) deep. The natural dam was under great stress.

In June 1841, the dam burst. Water raced through the Indus Valley. The flood was close to 100 feet (30 m) high. Rushing water scoured away everything in its path. Whole villages were wiped out.

View of Nanga Parbat, the peak where the rockslide originated.

## NATURAL DAMS CAUSE SERIOUS FLOODING

Natural dams form after rainstorms, rapid snowmelt, and earthquakes. Landslides cause rock, dirt, clay, and other debris to block a river. These natural dams are less stable than human-made dams. They often hold back more water, too. This combination can create disastrous flooding. If a natural dam breaks, waters flood the landscape downstream.

Image showing the rockslide dam and extent of the backup.

0  3  6
Kilometers

Three hundred miles (482 km) downstream, an entire army was reportedly drowned. No one knows how many people died in all. Experts say the Indus River flood of 1841 had the greatest release of water in recorded history.

# 500
**Army members reportedly drowned in the Indus River flood.**

- An earthquake caused a rockslide that dammed the Indus River.
- When the dam burst, a wall of water scoured the Indus Valley.
- Whole villages were wiped out by the rushing waters.
- People drowned as far as 300 miles (482 km) downstream.

# Flooding Leaves 80 Percent of New Orleans Underwater

Floods can result from all types of storms. Very serious flooding often follows hurricanes. People on the Gulf Coast of the United States learned this firsthand in August 2005.

In the hours and days after Hurricane Katrina, flooding affected coastal areas of Florida, Mississippi, and Louisiana. Worst

People waiting on their roof to be rescued.

hit was the city of New Orleans. It was especially at risk for flooding because the average elevation is six feet (1.8 m) below sea level. At first, levees and seawalls held the water back. Engineers worried, though, that storm surges would send water over the levees.

Storm surges from the gulf were massive. Water began to spill

## RESCUERS SEARCH THE CITY

Rescuers saved tens of thousands of people trapped by New Orleans flooding. Leading the effort was the Coast Guard. Using boats and helicopters, officials plucked people off rooftops. Ordinary citizens with boats joined in, navigating streets as though they were rivers. The Superdome was set up as a shelter. It housed as many as 25,000 people.

View of the 17th Street Canal breach that flooded the Orleans Parish neighborhood.

over some levees. It seeped through others, causing them to collapse. Because of failing levees, 80 percent of New Orleans was flooded. Entire neighborhoods were underwater. People scrambled to the roofs of their homes to escape rising water. Damages from the storm and flooding topped $100 billion.

Some experts believe better levees could have prevented the flooding. After floodwaters receded, new levees were planned and built. They were designed and constructed to hold back large storm surges.

## 20
**Depth of water in feet (6 m) in some parts of New Orleans.**

- New Orleans is at risk of flooding because much of it is below sea level.
- The city is protected by a system of levees and seawalls.
- Hurricane Katrina created massive storm surges that caused levees to fail.
- 80 percent of the city was flooded.

# Italian Art and Literature Lost in Arno River Flood

The Arno River in Italy has flooded more than 50 times since 1177. The worst flood was in November 1966. Heavy rains fell. The Arno swelled. Water levels peaked on November 4, flooding the city of Florence. In some places, water reached 10 feet (3 m) above street level. Mud, debris, oil, and sludge flowed through the city streets. At times, the water moved at 45 miles per hour (72 km/hr) through the historic center of Florence.

Thousands of homes and businesses were damaged or destroyed. Thirty-five people died. The water also reached galleries and libraries containing priceless works of art and literature from the Renaissance era. The flood damaged or ruined 1,500 sculptures and paintings. Many important manuscripts were also destroyed.

Since 1966, work has been done to help protect Florence from future floods. However, the Arno River is unpredictable. Some people believe that Florence could flood again, destroying even more homes and historic treasures.

Carmine Square in Florence after the flood.

# 1.5 million

**Approximate number of books that were underwater in Florence's Biblioteca Nazionale.**

- In early November 1966, the Arno River began to rise as a result of steady rain.
- The river flooded the streets of Florence with mud, oil, and other debris.
- Many priceless works of art and literature were lost.

A crucifix by the artist Cimabue from 1288 was nearly destroyed. It has been partially restored.

## MUD ANGELS RESCUE ITALIAN TREASURES

After the flood, many volunteers picked through the mud and muck to see what they could save. These included college students who were visiting Italy. Some were from the United States. They helped the Italians rescue many old books and scrolls. Many of these works have since been restored. Because of their efforts, the volunteers were called the Mud Angels.

13

# 6

# Three Rivers in Central China Overrun Their Banks

In 1929 and 1930, Central China experienced a severe drought. Then, in 1931, the region was hit by an unusual amount of rain. As much rain fell in July as usually fell over a year and a half. The Yellow, Yangtze, and Huai rivers flooded. In some places, water rose 90 feet (27 m) higher than normal.

As the rivers overran their banks, poorly built dikes burst. An area the size of England was left underwater. Acres of farmland were destroyed. Countless farm animals perished. There was also a massive human toll. Thousands drowned during flooding. More people died from the disease and famine that followed. In all, between 2 and 4 million people lost their lives.

THE ILLUSTRATED LONDON NEWS,

*The Copyright of all the Editorial Matter, both Engravings and Letterpress, is Strictly Reserved in Great Britain, the Colonies, Europe, and the United States of America.*

SATURDAY, SEPTEMBER 19, 1931.

FLOODS IN WHICH SEVERAL MILLIONS OF HUMAN BEINGS PERISHED: HANKOW STREETS UNDER WATER.

A 1931 London newspaper showing flooded streets in Hankow, China.

# 50 million

**People affected by the flooding, a quarter of China's population at the time.**

- In 1931, central China received an unusual amount of rainfall.
- The Yellow, Yangtze, and Huai rivers all overflowed their banks.
- An area the size of England was left underwater during flooding.
- Between 2 and 4 million people died from drowning, disease, and famine.

## CHINESE GOVERNMENT ACTS TO PREVENT FUTURE FLOODING

Central China has experienced many devastating floods throughout history. To prevent future disasters, China built the Three Gorges Dam on the Yangtze River. It was completed in 2006. The dam is 1.5 miles (2.4 km) across and 610 feet (186 m) high. It is designed to give officials more control over the river. While needed, the project did have a downside. More than 1 million people from 1,200 towns and villages were displaced.

# Dikes Give Way in Vietnam's Red River Delta

The Red River Delta is in northern Vietnam. It is an important area for rice production. In 1971, catastrophic flooding destroyed rice crops and many human lives.

Heavy rain fell between July 1 and August 20 of that year. The amount of rainfall was double what was normal. In the past, a series of dikes had protected rice fields and homes in the delta. Water had sometimes reached the tops of dikes, but it usually lowered right away. In the summer of 1971, however, the water level remained at flood stage for 55 straight days.

The dikes were under extreme stress. Eventually, four gave way. Water poured into the flat Red River Delta. The floodwater covered 1,737 square miles (4,500 sq km) of rice land. Between 35 and 45 percent of the rice crop that fall was lost. As much as 20 percent of livestock in the region died. Up to 100,000 people lost their lives. Many thousands more lost crops and homes. The flood also caused severe erosion and other environmental problems. Vietnam was forced to import more food than usual to feed its people.

# 75

**Percent of Vietnam's agricultural land that lies in the Red River Delta.**

- Rainfall during the summer of 1971 was twice the normal amount.
- Red River water levels were at flood stage for 55 days in a row.
- Four dikes protecting the Red River Delta failed.
- Approximately 100,000 people died in the flood.

# Flooding Mississippi Leaves Seven US States Underwater

The Great Mississippi River Flood of 1927 is the most destructive in US history. But the flooding actually began the year before. Late in the summer of 1926, it rained across the entire Mississippi River Valley. From the Appalachian Mountains in the east to the Rocky Mountains in the west, showers fell. And they kept falling. Rainfall totals for the year were ten times the annual average.

## $1 billion
### Amount of damage caused by the flood.

- Heavy rain fell across the Mississippi River Valley in the summer and fall of 1926.
- By winter, tributaries of the Mississippi began to flood.
- Rain continued into 1927 and levees along the Mississippi River failed.
- Parts of seven states were left underwater by flooding.

People had to live in camps on the levees for months until the water receded.

By winter, many tributaries of the Mississippi had flooded their banks. The Mississippi River itself was at risk of flooding.

Before 1927, the US Army Corps of Engineers had built a system of levees along the Mississippi. This system was meant to handle high water levels. But in March 1927, floodwaters from tributaries helped breach some levees. Rain continued to fall. More levees broke. Water poured through these breaks.

Parts of seven states were left underwater during flooding. Illinois, Missouri, Kentucky, Tennessee, Arkansas, Mississippi, and Louisiana were all affected. Floodwaters covered over 26,000 square miles (67,340 square km). The Mississippi River was more like a lake in some places, stretching 70 miles (113 km) across.

The flood affected close to 1 million people. Hundreds died. Another 637,000 were left homeless. The water did not recede until late summer.

# Dam Failure Wreaks Destruction along China's Ru River

In early August 1975, Typhoon Nina hit the south coast of China. It dumped massive amounts of rain. Over three days, more than three feet (1 m) of precipitation fell. These showers caused the Ru River to rise. The river was held back by the Banqiao Dam. This structure was built in the 1950s to prevent flooding. But during the record rains in August 1975, reservoir water levels reached the top of the Banqiao Dam. The dam weakened, and disaster seemed near.

On the night of August 8, a line of people atop the dam tried to save it. For a while, it looked like they would be successful. The water level even appeared to go down. Then the dam broke. Water burst through and roared downstream. The surge of water was more than 6 miles (10 km) wide and over 10 feet (3 m) high in some places. Waves raced downriver at more than 30 miles per hour (50 km/h).

The path of Typhoon Nina in 1975.

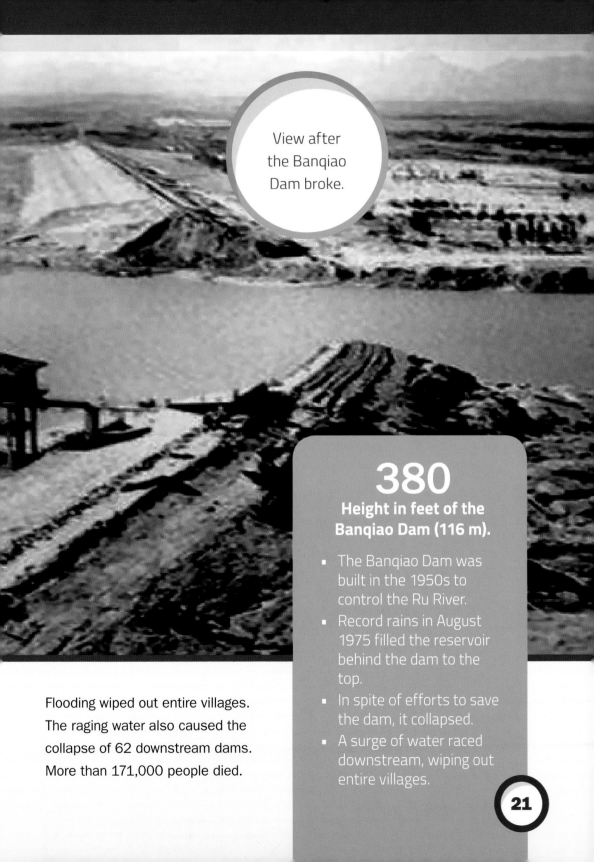

View after the Banqiao Dam broke.

# 380
**Height in feet of the Banqiao Dam (116 m).**

- The Banqiao Dam was built in the 1950s to control the Ru River.
- Record rains in August 1975 filled the reservoir behind the dam to the top.
- In spite of efforts to save the dam, it collapsed.
- A surge of water raced downstream, wiping out entire villages.

Flooding wiped out entire villages. The raging water also caused the collapse of 62 downstream dams. More than 171,000 people died.

# 10

# Machhu Dam Collapse in India Causes Catastrophic Loss

In August 1979, monsoon rains fell over western India. It rained for ten days straight. Behind the 2.5-mile-long (4 km) Machhu Dam, water levels rose. On August 11, water began to spill over the top. The earthen dam collapsed. A wall of water as tall as 30 feet (9 m) thundered through the densely populated valley below.

Downstream, people in rural villages and the city of Morbi did not know what was coming. The flash flood washed away buildings, cars, and animals. No one knows how many people died. Some estimates say between 5,000 and 10,000

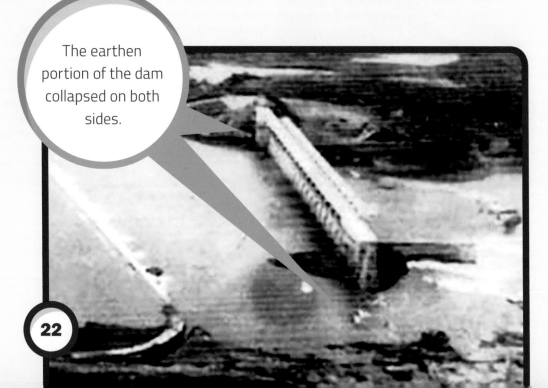

The earthen portion of the dam collapsed on both sides.

were killed. Others believe that number was closer to 25,000. Many people who survived had to rebuild their homes.

After the devastating event, India's government claimed the disaster was an act of God. However, an investigation found that the dam had been poorly designed. The government covered up this real reason for the dam's failure for 30 years.

## DESIGN FLAW LEADS TO MASS DESTRUCTION

The Machhu Dam was an earthen dam completed in 1978. It included floodgates. They were installed to release water during periods of heavy rain. Opening the floodgates relieves some of the pressure on a dam. However, the floodgates on the Machhu Dam were not large enough. In August 1979, water collected behind the dam faster than it was released. Eventually it rushed over the top of the dam and the dirt gave way.

# 5
### Miles downstream (8 km) Morbi is from the Machhu Dam.

- The Machhu Dam gave way on August 11, 1979, following monsoon showers.
- A wall of water caused major damage in rural villages and the city of Morbi.
- As many as 25,000 people died in the disaster.
- The government covered up the reason for the dam's collapse.

Illustration showing before and after the dam burst.

# Houston Submerged Following 50+ Inches of Rain

Floods caused by hurricanes are often very serious. The flooding that followed Hurricane Harvey in August 2017 was no exception. Between August 26 and August 30, the storm dumped rain on the US Gulf Coast states of Texas and Louisiana.

Houston, Texas, was one of the hardest-hit cities. The area received over 50 inches (127 cm) of rain. The result was widespread flooding. Residents fled their homes as the water rose. More than 30,000 people moved into shelters. At one point, there were about 240 shelters open for flood victims. The convention center in Houston served 7,500 people.

Thousands of other people were not able to make it to shelters. They were stranded by the flood. The 911 call center in Houston received 56,000 calls for help in the hours after the flooding began. In many places, emergency vehicles could not reach victims because the roads were

An aerial view of Port Arthur after the flooding.

# 27 trillion

**Gallons of water that fell on Texas and Louisiana over six days.**

- Hurricane Harvey caused severe flooding in Texas and Louisiana.
- More than 50 inches (127 cm) of rain fell on Houston.
- Widespread flooding forced residents to move to shelters.
- Other people were stranded by the floodwaters and had to be rescued.

flooded. Some people were rescued by officials in helicopters. Others were rescued by people in boats.

Adding to the disaster, two reservoirs in Houston reached capacity and began to overflow. Engineers were concerned that the unusual amount of water would cause the dams to fail. To relieve the pressure on the dams, engineers released water from the reservoirs. That sent additional water into streets already flooded by rain.

More than 80 people died. Losses were estimated at $75 billion. The Houston flooding is considered one of the worst weather-related disasters in US history.

# China Uses Yellow River as Weapon of War

In 1938, China and Japan were at war. The Japanese army was advancing westward across China. To stop the Japanese, the Chinese Nationalist government ordered troops to destroy dikes along the Yellow River. Officials believed the survival of the nation was worth the damage the flood would cause.

The muddy water was set free. It plunged into the valley below.

The Japanese army was temporarily cut off. But the action came at a high cost. The free-flowing river, combined with summer rain, flooded 21,000 square miles (54,390 sq km) of agricultural land. This area in Central China was densely populated. Most of the people living there did not get any warning of the coming flood.

Many thousands of people drowned in the flooding. Thousands more died from the disease and famine that followed. Four million people were left homeless.

Without the dikes to control water levels, the Yellow River continued to flood for the next several years. It even changed its course. It wasn't until 1947 that the river was once again under human control.

Families left homeless line up to receive assistance.

中央賑濟委員會第七救濟區
救濟黃災第一隊

# 8,000
**Approximate number of people who died in the Yellow River Flood of 1938.**

- Dikes along the Yellow River were destroyed to stop the Japanese during wartime.
- Floodwaters covered 21,000 square miles (54,390 sq km).
- 4 million people were left homeless.

## THINK ABOUT IT

Throughout the war between China and Japan (1937–1945), both sides used water as a weapon. Do you believe the desire to win the war justified the loss of life?

# Staying Safe If There Is a Flood

- Depending on where you live, floods might happen at any time of the year. Flood events might happen slowly or very quickly. Know the flood risks where you live.

- Even small amounts of fast-moving water can be dangerous. Six inches (15 cm) of running water can knock a person over. One foot (.3 m) of rushing water can move a car. Avoid walking or driving through floodwater.

- In the event of a flash flood, move to higher ground as fast as possible.

- In the event of flooding, stay tuned to radio, television, and social media. Follow all evacuation orders issued by firefighters and police. Know where to go for evacuation.

- If you live in an area prone to flooding, work with your family to make an evacuation plan. The plan should include how to find or communicate with friends and family after an evacuation. Identify at least two ways to leave the area.

- Be ready to evacuate on short notice. Work with your family to make a checklist of items to have ready if you must leave quickly. Be sure to include medicines and food.

- If you have a pet, know how you'll transport the animal during an evacuation. Pet food should be on your evacuation checklist.

# Glossary

**breach**
A break in a wall or barrier.

**debris**
Loose materials that are the result of something being broken or destroyed.

**dike**
A wall or mound built to protect against flooding.

**earthen dam**
A dam or barrier made of compacted soil to hold back water.

**famine**
Widespread shortage of food.

**flash flood**
A sudden rush of rapidly flowing water, usually the result of heavy rain.

**flood stage**
The point at which a body of water reaches extreme levels with risk of overflowing.

**infrastructure**
The structures a country needs to function, including dams, canals, roads, and bridges.

**levee**
A mound of earth material built up along the banks of a body of water.

**Renaissance era**
A time of great art, literature, and learning in Europe. The Renaissance started in the 1300s and lasted into the 1600s. The word Renaissance means rebirth.

**reservoir**
A human-made lake created by building a dam to hold back water.

**silt**
The fine materials, such as sand or dirt, carried by water and deposited as sediment.

**storm surge**
Rising sea levels as a result of a storm.

**tributaries**
Creeks, rivers, or streams that flow into larger bodies of water.

# For More Information

## Books

Edwards, Erika. *Levees and Seawalls.* Technology Takes on Nature. New York: Gareth Stevens Publishing, 2017.

Elkins, Elizabeth. *Investigating Floods.* Investigating Natural Disasters. North Mankato, MN: Edge Books, 2017.

Farndon, John. *Extreme Fires and Floods.* When Nature Attacks. Minneapolis: Hungry Tomato, 2017.

Spilsbury, Louise, and Richard Spilsbury. *Top 10 Worst Floods.* Nature's Ultimate Disasters. New York: Power Kids Press, 2017.

# Index

## About the Author

Laura Perdew is an author, writing consultant, and former middle school teacher. She writes fiction and nonfiction for children, including many titles for the education market. Laura lives and plays in Boulder, Colorado.

**READ MORE FROM 12-STORY LIBRARY**

Every 12-Story Library Book is available in many fomats. For more information, visit 12StoryLibrary.com